T0197508

Balance, Strength and Flexibility for Those with ADHD:

Key components for mental
and physical fitness

Kari Lewis, Ed.D.

Archway Publishing books may be ordered through booksellers or by contacting:

Archway Publishing
1663 Liberty Drive
Bloomington, IN 47403
www.archwaypublishing.com
844-669-3957

ISBN: 978-1-6657-4498-0 (sc)
ISBN: 978-1-6657-4499-7 (e)

Library of Congress Control Number: 2023910223

Print information available on the last page.

Archway Publishing rev. date: 07/10/2023

TABLE OF CONTENTS

"The mind is everything; what you think you become." - Socrates

Dedicated to my husband Stanley, and all my clients.
With a special thanks to Kirk for his quote and
to Amanda for her thorough review.

INTRODUCTION

Kari Lewis has over thirty years' experience working as an educator, consultant, and board-certified coach. She has been a professor, classroom teacher, educational consultant, parent workshop facilitator, teacher trainer, and program innovator.

During the summers of 1995 and 1996, Dr. Lewis was the educational coordinator for the Multimodal Treatment Study for Children with/without attention deficit hyperactivity disorder at Duke University. This national study is recognized world-wide as one of the foremost research studies examining the most effective treatment for children with ADHD.

For the past 26 years, Dr. Lewis has been in private practice as an ADHD coach for children and adults. She has particular expertise in coaching children to improve time management, organization, and planning for tests and projects. She also specializes in coaching working adults, stay-at-home moms, college students, and highly motivated professionals with ADHD. From 1987 - 2021, Dr. Lewis was a professor of physical education at a major university where she taught over five different activity courses along with adapted physical education, nutrition, exercise and weight management, and women's health issues.

ADHD

"No one thing should ever define your individual worth. You are strong and can evolve every day." – Kirk Stewart

ADHD is a condition that affects millions of children and about 4.4% of the adult population (Kessler, et al., 2006). ADHD arises from difficulties in the brain with regulation and uptake of two main neurotransmitters, dopamine and epinephrine. Many areas of the brain may be affected by this regulation and uptake of neurotransmitters.

Diagnostic and Statistical Manual (DSM) V - Diagnostic Criteria for ADHD (cdc.gov)

1. Hyperactivity and Impulsivity: Six or more symptoms of hyperactivity-impulsivity for children up to age 16 years, or five or more for adolescents age 17 years and older and adults; symptoms of hyperactivity-impulsivity have been present for at least 6 months to an extent that is disruptive and inappropriate for the person's developmental level:

- Often fidgets with or taps hands or feet, or squirms in seat.
- Often leaves seat in situations when remaining seated is expected.
- Often runs about or climbs in situations where it is not appropriate (adolescents or adults may be limited to feeling restless).
- Often unable to play or take part in leisure activities quietly.
- Is often "on the go" acting as if "driven by a motor".
- Often talks excessively.
- Often blurts out an answer before a question has been completed.
- Often has trouble waiting their turn.
- Often interrupts or intrudes on others (e.g., butts into conversations or games).

Treating ADHD is very important because of the impact that ADHD can have on many areas of life such as education, career, relationships, and health. Adult manifestations of ADHD include poor time management, difficulty initiating and completing tasks, flexibility in moving from one task/activity to another, procrastination, avoiding tasks that require attention, low frustration tolerance (e.g., changing jobs and/or relationships frequently), and impulsive aggressive behavior that tends to be verbal (Weiss,

Hechtman & Weiss, 1999). Additionally, health problems such as dependence on alcohol, drugs, and nicotine, heart disease, and obesity are correlated outcomes of ADHD (2021 chadd.org). Due to the high prevalence of ADHD and associated risks, strategies and tools to help maintain a healthy and balanced life are very important.

Among the adults that I work with, common complaints are: an inability to start work, not knowing when to take a break and/or taking a break for too long. Other complaints include difficulty in prioritizing tasks, difficulty in judging how long something will take, a willy nilly approach to school and work, and feeling overwhelmed with email correspondence and an inability to consistently balance work and home life. Furthermore, many clients continue to exhibit sleep problems into adulthood and the inability to avoid distractions, restlessness, and anxiety.

Here are some examples of these difficulties:

1. Pam moves from job to job after only about 6 months to a year in a position. She has revealed that she's easily bored and will get to a point where work piles up and it's easier to move on to a new job than to attempt to get on top of the current workload.

2. Alex, a college student, was attending a four-year university and was put on academic probation after his first semester. He chose to withdraw from the semester for psychological reasons. He reported that there came a time (about two weeks into the semester) when he felt behind, overwhelmed, and unable to keep up. At that point in time he stopped attending classes and only showed up to take a quiz or exam. Now he's transferred to a community college and is taking two classes which are two days/week. He's using a planner but doesn't utilize it fully. For example, each day he could write in his planner the assignments that are due and specific things that he needs to study, yet he's still attempting to hold all that information in his head or go back and forth repeatedly to Blackboard (an academic program where students look up information relevant to their courses) in order to find out what's due.

CHAPTER 2

The Relationship between Physical Fitness and Mental Cognition

"Growing pains: physical and mental, are part of the process." – Kirk Stewart

Mental health is essential for leading a healthy and balanced life. It helps people cope with stress, build relationships, and make positive decisions. It can also be affected by physical and environmental factors such as genetics, lifestyle, and social environment. Mental health can be improved with a variety of treatments, including medicine, cognitive behavioral therapy, talk therapy, and lifestyle changes.

Physical Fitness is a measure of the body's ability to function efficiently and effectively in work and leisure activities, and to meet emergency situations.

Carl Cotman, Professor of Neurology and Founding Director of the Institute for Brain Aging and Dementia at the University of Indiana, reported findings on exercise and its positive effects on health about twenty years ago (Cotman and Berchtold, 2002).

"We have been investigating possible behavioral interventions that may aid the brain in aging successfully. We suggest that exercise and environmental enrichment can have beneficial effects on brain function and health. Our findings suggest that exercise and Brain Derived Neurotrophic Factor (BDNF), a trophic factor known to support neuron survival and plasticity, is induced with a few days of voluntary running in animal studies." (https://mind.uci.edu/)

In simple terms, exercise can increase the proteins that help with the development of neurons and their survival. This may translate into better academic performance.

In a meta-analysis examining the relationship between physical activity and cognition, Sibley and Etnier (2003) reported a positive relationship for children ages 4-18. They reported that this suggests a relationship between physical fitness and cognitive outcome during the developmental years of life. Eight cognitive measurement categories (perceptual skills, achievement, verbal tests, math tests, memory developmental level/academic readiness and IQ) were assessed. Physical activity was related to cognitive performance in all the assessments except for memory.

Since the Sibley and Etnier (2003) meta-analysis, several other researchers (Kamijo, et al., 2011, and Rain, et al., 2013) have reported a strong relationship between aerobic fitness and various memory assessments for children. Although physical educators may only have anecdotal reports, they have known for many years that physical activity helps students be more attentive and intentional in the classroom.

In his book, Spark, (2008) Ratey, refers to the three levels in which exercise improves learning. These three levels are:

1. It's the catalyst for new nerve cells being developed from stem cells in the hippocampus. Advances in neuroscience have shown that new cells can be produced.

2. Exercise helps improve alertness and motivation by increasing neurotransmitters.

3. Exercise encourages the wiring together of nerve cell which is the basis for new information.

More recently, Blomstrand and Engvall (2021) reviewed the literature on the effects of exercise on learning and memory. Their investigation looked at studies indexed in PubMed and published between 2009 and 2019. Their review indicated that aerobic exercise improves learning and memory in young adults.

Although there is no empirical evidence to support the correlation between improved mental well-being (balance, strength and flexibility) and physical well-being (balance, strength and flexibility), there is support from philosophers, scientists, and therapists to support the connection between mind and body. John Ratey (2008) states that "Exercise balances neurotransmitters and keeping your brain in balance could change your life." Kelly McGonigal, in the Science of Willpower (2012) suggests "broadening your approach to the whole body." Research suggests that the confidence and ease of movement that we have physically can affect our mental/emotional state.

CHAPTER 3
Components of Physical Fitness

There are 5 components of physical fitness: muscle strength, muscle endurance, cardiorespiratory endurance, body composition, and flexibility https://www.acsm.org/education-resources/books/ACSMs-Fitness-Assessment-Manual

This book will focus on two of the components of fitness: muscle strength and flexibility. The third component, balance, is generally referred to as a skill related component of fitness.

Definitions:

Muscle strength - the ability of a muscle to exert force for a short period of time or for a few repetitions (i.e., not more than about 30 seconds and no more than about 10 repetitions).

Flexibility - The range of motion (ROM) at a joint.

Balance - The ability to maintain the body's center of mass above the base of support.

The relationship between physical fitness and mental cognition is well documented. Although there is no current research to support that improving physical strength, balance and flexibility will improve those same mental constructs, it does seem conceivable that it does happen. For example, David Goggins (2018) discusses emotional/mental calluses. Goggins participated in many endurance events and pushed himself to physical exhaustion, yet he was able to mentally push beyond the physical threshold of pain and persevere with many endurance events. He describes his ability to push himself physically to the point that he grew mentally stronger.

CHAPTER 4

Mental Balance

Avoid the lure of the highs and lows and strive for the valuable middle ground.

Wallace (2006) states: Emotional balance is the result of the balance between the purposeful action, attentional and cognitive balance. When we set realistic goals and commit ourselves to their achievement, we keep our expectations under control and focus on what really matters. Emotional balance is a natural result of the balance between desires, thoughts, and actions. Having a good emotional balance does not imply assuming an indifferent and cold attitude, but being aware of the emotions and feelings we are experiencing, understanding their influence, and being able to manage them and express them assertively.

Additionally, emotional balance is being able to determine what's important and then scheduling time for those things. It's also important to balance the effort and energy you'll put into tasks. If you schedule too many things to accomplish in one day, you'll likely run out of time and energy to complete everything.

Those with ADHD often go from one extreme to another and find it difficult to stay in that middle ground of feeling balanced. For example, someone with ADHD might notice at 11:00pm that the bathroom needs cleaning and they'll stay up all night to clean the bathroom. On the other hand, they might normally never do anything to tidy up the bathroom or do other menial tasks daily.

Balance can exist when you're able to set boundaries in your life. Boundaries exist in several forms: you can have time boundaries, physical boundaries and mental boundaries.

ADHD and Boundaries

Attention, time management and organization are just some of the areas in which someone with ADHD can have a difficult time setting boundaries. Setting a boundary with attention might mean being able to put on your blinders and attend to a task or assignment for a given amount of time (i.e., the time boundary). Telling a friend you'll be at their house at 6:00 pm and then figuring out what time you need to start preparing, to drive there, etc. is being able to set a time management boundary. Finally, establishing a place for everything in your car, house and office is setting a physical boundary(ies) around the organization of items.

Setting emotional/mental boundaries is also very important and will be discussed later in this chapter.

3 TYPES OF BOUNDARIES

Definition: a line that marks the limits of an area; a dividing line.

Physical boundaries - This is my house, this is my body, this is my desk, this is the physical space around me when I'm in public. Your house, dorm room, office space, car, etc. all provide a physical boundary. You can also establish a physical boundary with your body. You can decide who can be in your physical space, how close you want a person to be, and whether or not it's OK for people to touch you.

A. Background information about physical boundaries

Workspaces at school, work and home can be modified to suit your style of concentration. Many people with ADHD love the idea of being collaborative and having many others around. However, having others close by when trying to complete work might actually be a distraction. A client states that if it's a friend nearby she might be more likely to lose focus because of distracted conversation. However if it's a colleague nearby they might have a similar purpose and help keep each other on track.

Having an office with open space might be the worst thing for those with ADHD. It's a learning process to determine the physical boundaries you need in order to avoid distractions. Additionally, it's a learning process to determine how much time you'll spend with family and friends in relationships. It's important to know this in order to keep the balance with other areas of your life.

Being able to set physical boundaries with friends, family and sexual partners might be difficult because of distraction, impulsivity and low self esteem.

In a recent study funded by Harvard Business School, findings showed that open office spaces with limited spatial boundaries actually decreased the volume of face-to-face interaction significantly, by approximately 70%. And virtual interaction, via email and instant messenger, increased.

The study suggests that employees don't feel they can speak out loud in open offices because they might distract their coworkers. Instead of open discussions, employees remain at their desk and communicate with coworkers via online messaging.

B. Examples of clients that lack physical boundaries

Clara asked to have her study desk set up to face her sister's desk. The proximity of her sister's desk, plus having her sister so close is creating a distraction. It takes Clara 2-3 times longer than necessary to complete her homework.

Gabe's wife likes him to sit with her at night and watch TV. Many times, Gabe will still have work to do at night so he sits beside his wife with his laptop and attempts to get work done. So far, he's been unsuccessful due to the distraction of his wife and her close physical proximity.

C. Examples of clients that practice physical boundaries

Janine has found that she must do her work-from-home job in the sunroom of her house. The sunroom has a door that she can shut so the cats and her mom can't enter without her getting up and opening the door. The room provides a lot of sunshine which is beneficial. Sunshine stimulates the hormone serotonin which helps to elevate mood and increase focus. Another benefit is that the windows of the room face a fence so there aren't any distractions from outside.

Chad has found that he needs to work in an interior office space at his office. If he works in the community/open space, he becomes too distracted by his colleagues and he doesn't get his work done. In the interior office, he can close his door and put on noise canceling headphones. There aren't any windows to see what's happening outside his space.

Carmen, a 12-year old client, asked if his parents could replace his current desk, which has many drawers, with a desk that is simply a large, flat space in which to put his laptop and a pad of paper. The desk with drawers becomes a distraction because he can fiddle around with the contents of the drawer. Another problem with a desk is that he can put things in drawers and then he forgets where he puts things. Storing things out of sight most likely requires long term memory and/or working memory. Long term memory is something that needs to be remembered after about 30 seconds. Working memory is information that must be retrieved in order to influence a behavior or to help make a decision.

Malcolm has established a co-working agreement with a friend. The two of them have an appointment three times a week to meet on Zoom for a brief check in, and then they do their individual work while maintaining the Zoom connection. This provides accountability and motivation to complete work.

D. Tools and strategies for developing and maintaining physical boundaries

1. Set reminders and/or use sticky notes to remind yourself to work in your new space .

2. Have a work or school buddy to help you be accountable in staying in your new space.

3. At the end of the work day or school day, be sure to clean up your space so that it's ready for the next day. If you fail to do that you might arrive at your space the next day and think that it's too messy or distracting and move to a spot that is lacking the physical boundaries that you need.

4. Identify and acknowledge where your boundaries exist.

5. Plan ahead to anticipate a need to set a boundary. For example, new flooring will be put in your home office. This will take an entire day. Plan ahead to have space in another room of the house or experiment ahead of time to see if working in a public space would be ok for you.

Emotional boundaries

A. Background information about emotional boundaries

Boundaries might be rigid, loose, somewhere in between, or even nonexistent. A complete lack of boundaries may indicate that we don't have a strong identity or are enmeshed with someone else.

Healthy boundaries are a crucial component of self-care. That's because "in work or in our personal relationships, poor boundaries lead to resentment, anger, and burnout" (Nelson, 2016). Those with ADHD may find it difficult to set emotional boundaries due to emotional dysregulation.

Emotional dysregulation refers to the inability of a person to control or regulate their emotional responses to certain stimuli. It's reported that over 50% of adults with ADHD have difficulty with emotional regulation (Barkley, 2015). When a person becomes emotionally dysregulated, they may react in an emotionally exaggerated manner to environmental and interpersonal challenges by displaying bursts of anger, crying, accusing, passive-aggressive behaviors, or by creating conflict. Emotional dysregulation can also mean that a person displays elation, joy, and laughter when it's an inappropriate response to a stimulus.

Located in the middle part of the brain is an area called the limbic system. This instinctual brain oversees the fear and stress responses, emotional memories, and the sense of smell. This is where the amygdala is located. The amygdala acts like a command center that communicates with the rest of your body through your nervous system. According to brain scans and neuroimage fMRI studies (functional magnetic resonance imaging), amygdala activity is also present in response to emotional facial expressions. It plays an important role in "defending" and keeping you safe within your comfort zone. Your amygdala scans your environment regularly in the same way that a smoke alarm would detect smoke. When you experience a negative emotion, its response is to sound the alarm to alert your hypothalamus.

Patients with ADHD tend to have smaller amygdala volumes. ADHD patients presented less activation in the area of the left frontal lobe than the controls. There was no amygdala activation when presenting the pleasant images, whereas bigger activation of the left amygdala was found in patients while presenting them unpleasant images. These results might suggest that lower emotional processing and less control of impulsivity is associated with a dysfunctional amygdala in ADHD patients. (Tajima-Pozo, et al., 2018)

Excessive amygdala activity is connected to post-traumatic stress disorder (PTSD) and anxiety disorders because it causes extreme reactions to emotional events, memories, emotional stimuli, and visual stimuli. Many of those with ADHD also experience anxiety (Kessler, 2006).

Risk-taking, common for those with ADHD, is also associated with the amygdala. The amygdala also keeps you stuck in the past. It influences fear conditioning and emotional memory. An overactive amygdala will lead to a state of chronic fear-based reactions and the constant subconscious activation of your emotional memory bank.

A. Examples of clients that lack emotional boundaries

Carly's mom complains about her disrespectful behavior and that Carly texts only when she needs money or is in a dire situation. Carly's mom has attempted to limit the time she spends with Carly because she feels emotionally drained each time. However, Carly's mom has agreed to allow Carly to go on a family trip because Carly used manipulative language to persuade her mom. "You always do this to me, you like Sasha and Carlos better (Carly's sister and brother).

Rita, a nanny, "judges" her day based on how much her nanny family praises her. If someone in the family praises her then she feels happy, sometimes even giddy. On the other hand, if there's no praise or she hears a statement that appears to be critical, she may feel unmotivated, and even depressed.

Singh, a college student, reacts like a twelve year old when his mom questions him about his grades, apartment cleanliness, and money. His reactions range from swearing at his mom to throwing things and hanging up the phone.

B. Examples of clients that practice emotional boundaries

- Caitlin has identified that spending time with her dad is a trigger and she becomes anxious when she's around him. She also quickly reverts to using immature body language (rolling her eyes, folding her arms, and avoiding eye contact) when she's around her dad. Caitlin now practices doing three to four cycles of square breathing multiple times per day. When she knows she's going to be around her dad, she does more cycles of square breathing and identifies a place where she can go to get away for a few minutes and breathe.

- Trevor knows that when he gets too hungry and/or is too tired that his emotions are more difficult to regulate, so he strives for 7 - 8 hours of sleep every day of the week and he makes sure he's got readily available (in the car, golf bag, etc.) snacks at all times. He recognizes that HALT (hungry, angry, lonely, tired) is a tool for self care and regulating his emotions. Trevor has recognized that if he has these unmet physiological needs that he's more likely to be distracted.

- Anisha has a work computer and a personal computer. She works from home and has a "workshop" about 200 feet from her house. The work computer stays in the workshop and the personal computer stays in the house in order to keep a boundary between home and work.

C. Tools and strategies for developing and maintaining emotional boundaries

- Dialectical behavioral therapy (DBT) specifically addresses many of the issues associated with setting boundaries. DBT helps people learn to better regulate themselves through a combination of these therapies such as mindfulness, distress tolerance, interpersonal effectiveness, and emotion regulation.

- Cognitive Behavioral Therapy (CBT) helps to change thinking patterns and unlearn unhealthy behaviors.

- ADHD coaching can help target individual behaviors and break down a method(s) to achieve the target behavior(s).

- Square breathing, meditation, yoga, and chanting all help to reduce disorder in the amygdala and therefore aid in regulating emotions.

Time boundaries - Being able to set a boundary around the time you'll allot to certain errands and committing to that time boundary. An example of lacking time boundaries is to say you'll be somewhere in 10 minutes and it's 20 minutes before you get there or letting tasks/chores and assignments go on and on without establishing a finish point. If your homework time is willy-nilly without planning, you always arrive late, you have difficulty planning when to start a meal, and/or you wake up and go to bed at different times every day then time boundaries are a problem for you.

A. Background and research on time management and time boundaries

In addition to the common symptoms of impulsivity and difficulty avoiding distractions, ADHD often presents with emotional dysregulation and mood instability, and although thought to be secondary issues, problems with time perception are considered to be a central symptom of ADHD (Weissenberger, 2021).

The concept of time is a mental and biological construct that is innate in many living organisms and includes the perception of time, time sequencing, and time reproduction. Observing the changes in the environment are how we keep track of time. The perception of time is directly associated with time processing, or the ability to record and estimate how much time is passing. Those with ADHD may lack the ability to avoid distractions and so they have a difficult time noting the changes in the environment. Additionally, because time is a biological construct, some people with ADHD fail to notice when they're hungry, tired, etc., so time passes without the need to stop and fulfill those biological needs. Ignoring these needs can lead to other health problems.

No single brain region has been identified as responsible for time perception. This function appears to be dispersed throughout the central nervous system and is intrinsically associated with brain connectivity and communication. Being able to estimate time and time perception appear to be two separate things. In MRI studies brain activity increases in the basal ganglia with time perception activities while the prefrontal cortex is the area of activity during time estimation tasks and that is dependent upon dopamine (Coull, 2011).

Weissenberger (2021) suggested that the connection between executive dysfunction and ADHD could be the cause of the deficit in the perception of time. Executive functions are those that control behaviors such as what to focus on, when and how to initiate something, and monitoring behavior to complete tasks.

Ptacek (2019) reports that practical approaches to time perception and its evaluation have shown that individuals with ADHD have difficulties in time estimation and discrimination activities as well as having the feeling that time is passing by without them being able to complete tasks accurately and well. Although ADHD has been associated with neurologic abnormalities in the mesolimbic and dopaminergic systems, recent studies have found that when individuals with ADHD are treated medically, their perception of time tends to normalize (Rosello, 2020) The relationship between ADHD and the perception of time requires greater attention. Further studies on time perception in ADHD with other abnormalities, including executive function, might involve approaches that refine the classification and diagnosis of ADHD and should include studies on its varied presentation in different age groups.

Differences in retrospective time estimates are observed among patients diagnosed with ADHD even when compared to those with other psychiatric disorders (Walg, 2017). Walg (2017) reviewed the literature pertaining to time perception as a central issue in time management for those with ADHD. Shifts in cognitive processing take time and for those with ADHD, the shifts may be slower and require more time for a transition between the shifts. The differences in time that is experienced by those with ADHD may be at the very root of ADHD-related symptoms given the importance of coordinated signals. Some of these differences include the feeling of time moving faster, which cause difficulties in prospective time tasks and inaccuracies in time estimation tasks. In this review of the literature, (Walg, 2017) the authors strongly recommend the inclusion of ADHD symptoms associated with time perception in the next revision of the Diagnostic and Statistical Manual of Mental Disorders (DSM) published by the American Psychiatric Association (APA).

A. Examples of clients that lack time boundaries

Gabe can't seem to get to his appointments on time, Hannah can't get her assignments turned in on time, and Cameron runs out of meds every month because he doesn't pick up his prescriptions on time.

Paul, a work at home programmer, has a difficult time completing his work. He's interrupted frequently by his wife and children. Each interruption provides the opportunity to get distracted and before he knows it, it's 5:00 pm and the work-day is over.

B. Examples of clients that practice time boundaries

Vinny uses a written planner to plan his daily appointments, Dex uses an app and his phone alarms to remind him when to stop playing Pokemon Go, and Aidan texts his ADHD coach when he goes to bed so that he's held accountable for his time.

Rolando, an attorney in private practice, found that when he answered a phone call it would take him 4-10 minutes to be able to return to what he'd been working on prior to the call. To avoid the time loss due to those transitions he made a voicemail recording that stated, "Mr. Floyd returns phone calls between 1 and 2:30 daily. He makes every effort to return calls within 24 hours." Setting this time boundary helped Rolando to manage his time and allowed him to be able to complete tasks required to run a solo practice.

Caleb, a programmer, has a kanban board taped to his at home office wall. He uses color coded post it notes to keep track of his "to-do's, working on and done" tasks. Additionally, he writes the amount of time (or estimated time) that it'll take to complete a task.

C. Tools and strategies for developing and maintaining time boundaries

Consistent use of a written planner, app or digital calendar can be very helpful. There is no universal best tool. Rather, it depends on the person and what will be the simplest tool to use. It may be helpful to have a few tools and rotate among them from time to time to avoid familiarity and the loss of novelty that can be attractive for those with ADHD.

Examples of tools to help with time boundaries:

1. Apps to act as reminders

2. Pin a post it note to your shirt with the time that you need to start or stop something.

3. Use virtual assistant technology, such as Alexa

4. Be realistic in estimating how long something will take to do.

5. Schedule flex time into your day. This is a segment(s) of time that is free time, but can be used if something comes up that is out of the ordinary. It's important to schedule your day, but allot the flex time so you can get everything completed.

CHAPTER 5

Physical Balance

Physical balance can transfer into balance in other areas of my life.

Balance is important to physical well-being. Maintaining good balance is critical to being able to continue to perform the activities we want to do and to help ensure as much independence as possible as we age. Training in a way to improve physical balance may be helpful in thinking about emotional balance.

Your body is always seeking balance. Although we're not aware of it, sensory input is giving our muscles information to help keep us balanced. For those with ADHD and other neurodevelopmental issues, deficits in motor control may be present and create difficulties in maintaining balance. Postural sway is an indicator of a person's ability to achieve and maintain balance. Postural sway is the movement we make while standing in an attempt to maintain balance. The more postural sway a person has, the more movement you will see as you observe them standing in place. The movement is generally a very gentle movement from side to side or in small circles.

The Romberg Test is a test to measure balance and postural sway. The testee stands with bare feet. She's then instructed to close her eyes and maintain balance for as long as possible. The degree of postural sway will cause balance to be disturbed.
https://www.physio-pedia.com/Romberg_Test

Impaired balance and increased postural sway are commonly reported in children with ADHD (Jansen, 2019). Schlee et al. (2012) examined the difference in balance and posture in children with and without ADHD. The difference in plantar pressure between the left foot and right foot in the ADHD group was greater than that observed in the control group. The average center of pressure jerk score of the right foot in the ADHD group was higher than that observed in the control group. A higher functional connectivity between the cerebellum and the right middle frontal gyrus (premotor cortex) and medial frontal gyrus (cingulate gyrus) was observed in the control group relative to the ADHD group. In the ADHD group, the difference in plantar pressure between the left and right foot was also negatively correlated with the beta-value within the middle frontal gyrus. The investigators concluded that children with ADHD had disturbance of balance as assessed by plantar pressure. The disturbances in posture, for those with ADHD, were associated with less brain communication between the cerebellum (the part of the brain that helps coordinate functions) and the premotor cortex (which is associated with motor movement and sensation).

Researchers (Fengl, et al. 2020) compared two treatment methods for postural sway in children with ADHD. Treatment one was methylphenidate (MPH) and the experimental group received MPH plus balance training. It was reported that the experimental group displayed a significant improvement in the symptoms and behavior associated with inattention than the group whose treatment consisted only of MPH (Fengl, et al., 2020).

Although postural sway and balance abnormalities are well documented in children, the adult population with ADHD was not included in the studies until Hove (2015) investigated the adult population. Hove, et al. (2015) investigated postural sway in an adult population with ADHD.

In their study, Hove et al. measured postural sway in adults with ADHD and controls, examining the relationship between sway and regional cerebellar gray matter volume. Thirty-two ADHD and 28 control participants completed various standing-posture tasks on a Wii balance board. The results indicated that "postural sway was significantly higher for the ADHD group compared to the healthy controls. Higher sway was positively associated with regional gray matter volume in the right posterior cerebellum (lobule VIII/IX)." Furthermore, they concluded that postural sway abnormalities are present in adults also, and that for the first time show a relationship between postural control abnormalities and the cerebellum in the adult group.

Based on the findings of these researchers, balance training is important for children and adults with ADHD.

Training for physical balance

If you've not been training for balance then start gradually. For all of these, be sure to switch feet and do balance activities on both the right and left sides.This is a list of increasingly difficult balance activities. Start your training with one or two of the balance activities below:

1. Stand on one foot with the other foot propped up on a step or low bench. Time how long you can keep your balance on one foot. Do this 5 times per day.

2. Balance on one foot while standing in line at the grocery store or in line for tickets, etc. Time how long you can keep your balance. Do this 5 times per day.

3. Walk on a flat line on a sidewalk or floor. Measure the distance that you're able to stay on the line. Do this 5 times per day.

4. Walk on a balance beam. Measure the distance that you're able to stay on the beam. Do this 5 times per day.

5. Walk forward with your eyes closed. Increase the distance that you walk in a relatively straight line. Do this 5 times per day.

6. Stand on a bosu ball. Time how long you can keep your balance. Do this 5 times per day.

7. Do any of the above with your eyes closed.

CHAPTER 6

Mental Strength

> "My mental strength is a muscle that I can train. My boundaries around space, time and feelings are worth respecting." – Amanda Rhode

David Goggins, an ultra-marathoner, Navy Seal, and war veteran, espouses pushing himself to the limit, both physically and mentally. He states, (pg 93) "...that's when I realized that not all physical and mental limitations are real, and that I had a habit of giving up way too soon." He goes on to talk about a "calloused mind" (page 101). His physical training was so intense that he had to find a way to move beyond the physical pain. That's when he developed a calloused mind strong enough to handle the physical pain.

Just as balance is important to your physical well-being, so is strength. Maintaining physical strength is critical to being able to continue to do the activities you want to do. Physical strength is defined as the ability to exert a force for a short period of time or for a few repetitions.

Training in a way to improve physical strength may be translated into improving mental strength.

For those with ADHD, deficient emotional self-regulation (DESR) is a common characteristic. DESR is the inability to regulate responses to certain emotions and/or to overreact to daily situations.

Mental Strength - Being able to bounce back following life challenges, setbacks and personal failures and to deal effectively with circumstances of life. How quickly can you return to equilibrium/homeostasis? Developing mental strength enhances self esteem and provides us with the knowledge that we can handle all things that come our way.

Mental strength can be displayed in many ways, and one way is being disciplined.

William A. McRaven, in his book, *Make your Bed* (page 111) states, "If you make your bed every morning, you will have accomplished the first task of the day. It will give you a small sense of pride and it will encourage you to do another task and another and another. By the end of the day, that one task completed will have turned into many tasks completed. Making your bed will also reinforce the fact that little things in life matter. If you can't do the little things right, you will never do the big things right. And, if you by chance have a miserable day, you will come home to a bed that is made—that you made—and a made bed gives you encouragement that tomorrow will be better."

Additionally, mental toughness has been defined as the company of one or more learned and inherited values, attitudes, emotions, cognitions and behaviors. These attributes impact the way an individual copes with pressures, stressors, challenges, and adversities in training and competitions (Slack, Meynard, Butt & Olusoga, 2015). Repeating these difficult actions can desensitize a person to perceived stressors.

Clough, Earle & Sewell (2002) have come up with four components otherwise known as "*The 4C's Model*" that can be trained through psychological skills training, which will help to build mental toughness.

> The 4 C's are:
>
> Control - People who are mentally tough are not afraid to take control or responsibility for the situation that they are in.
>
> Commitment - Mentally tough individuals involve themselves fully in what they are doing and always give maximum effort.
>
> Challenge - The person who is mentally tough views all stressful situations as being challenging and focuses on what can be gained from stressful situations.
>
> Confidence - The most mentally tough individuals have an immensely strong belief in their ability to achieve success.

The four Cs are the foundations of mental toughness. Researchers have also identified several traits and behavior that are associated with mental toughness. Some of these are persistence, self-belief, ability to focus, and an ability to maintain emotional control.

Practice for mental strength - It is well known that exercise increases serotonin. Low serotonin can lead to anxiety, fear and negative thoughts. So by increasing physical strength, mental strength can increase.

1. Make your bed! Start the day with one simple act of discipline. You may find that this is the thing that will begin a snowball effect for a day of discipline.

2. Exercise - After making your bed engage in at least 20 minutes of vigorous exercise. That means that you should be able to hear yourself breathe and it would be difficult to carry on a normal conversation because you would be slightly breathless.

3. Set daily, weekly and long term goals and keep track of when you accomplish the goal(s)

   - Remember that goals are more powerful if they are SMART goals. SMART stands for specific, measurable, achievable, realistic and time bound.

     - Example: I will be able to do 30 pushups by May 25 (10 weeks away).

4. Keep a journal or a document of your successes. That way when you're encountering a new challenge, you'll have past experiences to give you the confidence to persevere with the new challenge.

5. Practice visualization and use positive affirmations.

Athletes and musicians use visualization to "practice" their sport/activity while sitting, on a plane, listening to music, etc. When visualizing, use as many emotions as possible.

Example: If you have test anxiety and you're studying for the LSAT, then create an environment that looks like the actual test environment. Visualize what sounds you might hear, what people might be around you, etc. Give yourself the exact time constraints as will be used for the LSAT. Then visualize yourself confidently answering the questions and proceeding through the test with self assuredness and confidence.

6. Practice square breathing. Do 3-4 cycles of this to help decrease your heart rate and reduce anxiety.

    Inhale to the count of 4
    Hold your breath to the count of 4
    Exhale to the count of 4
    Hold your breath to the count of 4

7. Practice saying 3 positives for each negative.

    - The practice in behavior management is to give 3 positives for each negative encounter. This practice is also effective with self-talk. Additionally, it's important to use third person when doing this to avoid identifying yourself as a condition. Instead of saying "I'm stressed," say, "I'm feeling stressed."

        o   Example: If your name is Eduardo and the self-talk you use is, "I'll never be able to finish this project." Then the 3 positives could be: "Eduardo is capable of completing this project. Eduardo has the skills and ability to finish this project. Eduardo has felt like this before and he knows that he can complete this project."

8. Each day do something that is outside your comfort zone.

    - Practice using those neurons, brain cells, and muscles to do a difficult task. This could be an actual task such as cleaning the toilet or it could be making a phone call that is difficult, or requesting a meeting with a professor in a class that you're failing.

9. Practice mindfulness, meditation, and/or progressive muscle relaxation.

    A 6 minute progressive muscle relaxation
    https://www.youtube.com/watch?v=9x3tl81NW3w
    Daily Calm: 10 minute meditation
    https://www.youtube.com/watch?v=ZToicYcHIOU
    How mindfulness changes the emotional life of our brains
    https://www.youtube.com/watch?v=7CBfCW67xT8

10. Practice yoga

    There are many different levels of yoga and many different poses. Choose the ones that are comfortable for you. Then progress at a level that is challenging, yet still relaxing.

CHAPTER 7

Physical strength

"It is exercise alone that supports the spirit, and keeps the mind in vigor." – Cicero

A physical challenge can help you take control over other areas of your life, i.e., mental challenges.

David Goggins (pg 141) states, "Physical training is the perfect crucible to learn how to manage your thought process."

Practice for physical strength

1. Lift weights or do resistance exercises 3 - 6 days per week

    *   Select 1-2 lifts to develop each major muscle group.

    *   Major Muscle groups are:

        1. Pectorals - Chest
        2. Latissimus dorsi -Back
        3. Deltoids and trapezius - Shoulders
        4. Biceps - Front of arms
        5. Triceps - Back of arms
        6. Abdominals - Trunk
        7. Gluteals - Buttocks
        8. Quadriceps -Front of thighs
        9. Hamstrings - Back of thighs
        10. Tibialis anterior - Front of leg
        11. Gastrocnemius and soleus - Calf muscles

* Lift heavy enough so that you can complete about 4-10 repetitions per lift.

Muscle strengthening exercises

Pictured below is one lift (with a starting and stopping point) for each of the major muscles. These lifts can be performed by anyone, anywhere. They require no special equipment. Depending upon your level of experience and strength you can use your body weight, water bottle filled with sand or water, books, paint can, and/or weight to perform the lifts.

Pectorals - Chest press

Start with the weight on top of or near your chest. End with weight over your chest with your arms straight.

Chest press dumbell on chest

Chest press dumbell pressed over the chest

Latissimus dorsi - One arm row

Place your right knee on a bench or chair; your arm should be hanging straight down. End with your elbows bent and the weight over your chest.

One arm row arm hanging straight down

One arm row elbow bent

Deltoids and Trapezius - Overhead press

Hold a weight over your head with your elbows bent, then press the weight over your head and straighten your arms.

Weight over head with elbows bent

Weight over head with arms straight

Biceps - Bicep curl

Begin with arms straight and next to the sides of your body. Next, bend one arm to bring the weight up in front of your bicep or squeeze muscle if you are not using weights.

Right arm down, left arm bent

Right arm bent, left arm straight

Triceps - French press

Hold a weight behind your head with your elbows bent. Straighten your arms and raise the weight over head.

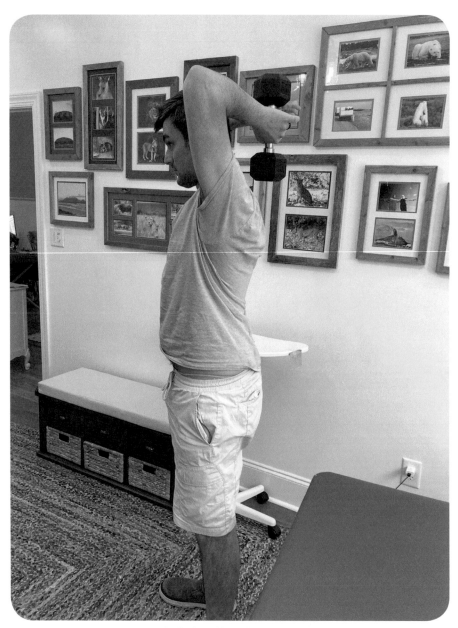

Weight behind head elbows bent

Arms straight overhead

Thighs and Gluteals - Squats

Stand with your feet shoulder width apart and feet flat on the floor. Bend your knees and slowly lower your buttocks as if you are going to sit in a chair. Keep your feet flat and knees pointing forward.

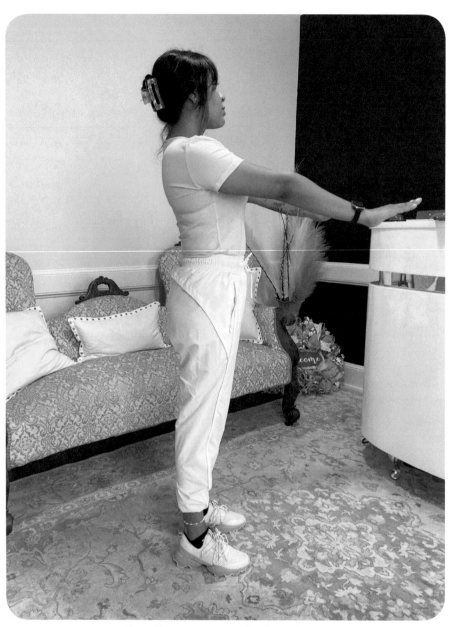

Standing arms stretched out front

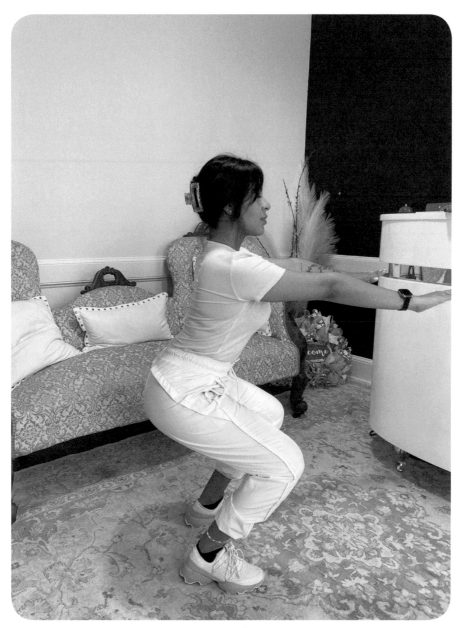

squatting

Tibialis anterior - Heel walking with toes up

Plant your heels on the ground with toes off the floor, and continue walking with toes off the ground.

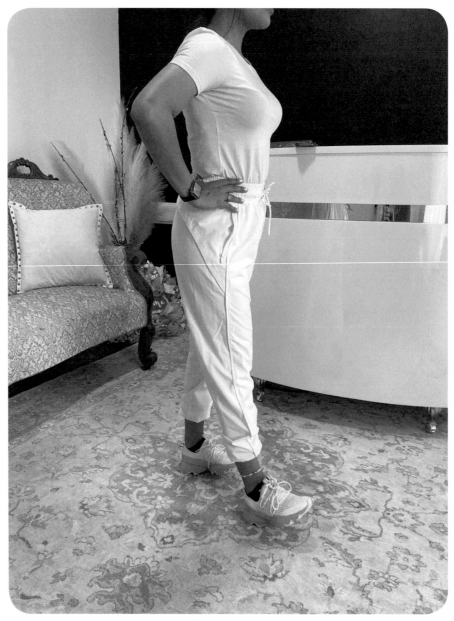

Standing right toe up

Standing left toe up

Gastrocnemius- Heel raise

Hold a weight in your left hand and hold onto a stable object with your right hand. Place the left ball of your foot on a step and raise up on the ball of your foot. Lower your left heel down as far below the step as possible. Repeat steps with the right leg.

Heel off edge of step

Raise up on toe

Abdominals - Plank on elbows and with straight arms

Start on the floor with palms to the side of your body near your shoulder, or if you are doing a forearm plank, position forearms to the side of your body. Press your body straight up while keeping your body straight and parallel to the floor. If you are doing a forearm plank, press upwards until your upper arms are straight and at a 90° angle to your forearms. Your body should be kept straight and parallel to the floor.

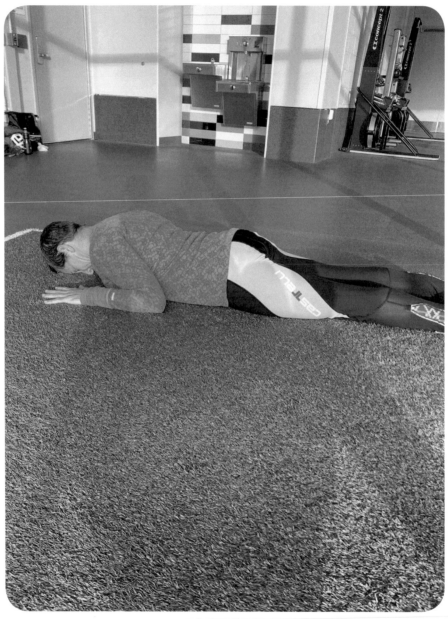

Lying flat

Plank with arms straight

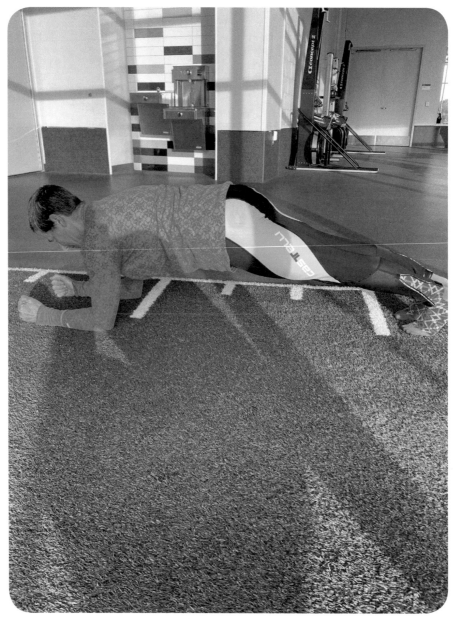

Plank on elbows

CHAPTER 8
Mental Flexibility

My creative mind helps me to be flexible in my thoughts and actions.

Mental Flexibility is the ability to adapt thinking and behavior in response to what's happening in the environment. It includes the ability to see another person's point of view, the ability to shift from one task to another, and the ability to generalize skills and behaviors. Cognitive flexibility is an important executive function that reflects our ability to shift thinking and to produce a steady flow of creative thoughts and answers as opposed to a regurgitation of the usual responses. The trait correlates with high-performance levels in intellectually demanding jobs (Spark 2008).

Dr. Lin at UNC (July 29, 2022 in Health Day Report) reported that kids with ADHD have less flexibility in the brain circuitry that allows for efficient brain shifting.

The following is an excerpt from The Beck Institute:

"The American psychiatrist Aaron Beck (1921-present), a founder of cognitive behavioral therapy (CBT), has also alluded to the problem of inflexibility through his discussion of 'cognitive distortions.' Beck, who worked chiefly with depressed patients, noticed that they often made allusions to troubling, catastrophic, and negative thoughts. Over time, he came to believe that such negative, irrational, exaggerated, rigid, and biased thoughts (i.e. cognitive distortions) are at the root of depression. The idea of flexibility shows itself in the CBT tradition particularly as it pertains to the common cognitive distortion known as 'all or nothing' thinking (a.k.a. 'black or white' thinking)."

In other words, psychological flexibility in the Acceptance and Commitment Therapy (ACT) (i.e., accepting life as it comes) framework pertains mainly to the person's commerce with the world, and is viewed as a person's ability to adapt to dynamic situational demands, effectively summon and direct their mental resources, shift perspective with agility, and balance competing desires and demands. Thus, psychological flexibility allows the person to calibrate their responses to the here-and-now situational demands, to focus their attention and direct their energy effectively, to be able to take the long term perspective even in the midst of emotional turmoil, and behave in ways that honor their core values and facilitate the attainment of their meaningful goals.

Although he expected his research into the psychoanalytic construct of depression to validate the tenets of psychoanalysis, Dr. Beck was surprised when his initial studies with depressed patients seemed to refute its underlying theories. His work with depressed patients led him to develop a new theory of depression, one focused on underlying negative beliefs associated with loss and failure, rather than the psychoanalytic theory that depression is the result of hostility turned toward the self and that depressed patients have an innate need to suffer. Dr. Beck's patients expressed spontaneous, negative thoughts, which he eventually termed "automatic thoughts." Adopting a collaborative role with his patients, Dr. Beck helped them evaluate the validity and utility of their automatic thoughts and cognitive distortions. He found that his patients' thoughts about a situation influenced their reactions—more so than the situation itself, a construct he termed the "cognitive model." He helped his patients change the way they thought about situations and engage in more adaptive behaviors, which helped them feel better. He also worked with them to address underlying maladaptive beliefs about themselves, others, the world, and the future. He called his new therapy "Cognitive Therapy," which was later termed Cognitive Behavior Therapy, or CBT.

Various groups representing a number of different perspectives (for example, operational, architectural, community, institutional, and individual resilience) use the term resilience. We define resilience as the ability to withstand, recover, and grow in the face of stressors and changing demands. Physical fitness is one pathway toward resilience because it is associated with many traits and attributes required for resilience. In addition, physical fitness confers resilience because regular exercise and/or physical activity induces positive physiologic and psychological benefits, protects against the potential consequences of stressful events, and prevents many chronic diseases (Deuster, 2013).

Practicing mental flexibility - keep in mind that all mental anguish has a beginning and an end. Practice "seeing " more and/or alternate solutions to problems. Write these down and discuss with someone else....get out of your own head!

Examples of statements from clients that lack mental flexibility:

1. I don't like my math teacher, therefore I won't study or do well in math.

2. I "read" the facial expression of an employer as negative, therefore I am afraid to ask for time off.

3. I quit my job because my email inbox became overwhelming.

Examples of clients that practice mental flexibility:

1. My alert for doing a homework assignment didn't go off so I'll need to accept the zero, but I'll continue with my plan for the day.

2. My tire had a bolt in it and I had to get to the service station so I'm going to be late to my doctor's appointment. I'll call and let the doctor know and see if I can show up late or if I'll need to reschedule.

CHAPTER 9

Physical Flexibility

Flexibility is the key to youth.

Flexibility is important to your physical well-being. Maintaining flexibility is critical to being able to continue to do the activities we want to do. Flexibility is defined as the range of motion around a joint. Activities that lengthen and stretch muscles can help you prevent injuries, back pain, and balance problems. A well-stretched muscle more easily achieves its full range of motion.

Youtube is a good source for videos on stretching. Here are a few:

<u>13 min. Full Body Stretch Routine For Tight Muscles| Beginner Friendly</u>

<u>8 Stretches You Should Do Everyday To Improve Flexibility</u>

https://www.healthline.com/health/benefits-of-flexibility

CHAPTER 10

Practice for Balance, Strength and Flexibility

According to Stephen Covey, "Only the disciplined are truly free. The undisciplined are slaves to moods, appetites, and passions."

Self-discipline is a muscle that gets stronger the more you flex it.

Suggested activities to improve all 3: balance, strength and flexibility.

Yoga
tai chi
pilates

Daily practice for the beginner - these can be incorporated into your daily routine

While waiting in line, stand on one foot.
While waiting in line, stand with your eyes closed and then try it on one foot.
While walking down a level sidewalk or in your yard walk a few feet with your eyes closed. And then practice walking a little further each time.
Stretch your hamstrings while putting on your shoes - hold the stretch 20-60 seconds.
Reach up to grab something from a top shelf (be sure it's not too heavy).
Avoid using a wheelbarrow when you can carry something instead.
Always use the stairs. Take two stairs at a time.

Advanced exercises to improve all 3: balance, strength and flexibility

Balance, strength and flexibility
https://www.youtube.com/watch?v=3sTAZE0WtAE

REFERENCE

American American College of Sports Medicine. (2021). ACSMs-Fitness-Assessment-Manual (6th ed.). Lippincott, Williams & Wilkins.

Barkley, R. A. (2015). Emotional dysregulation is a core component of ADHD. In R. A. Barkley (Ed.), *Attention-deficit hyperactivity disorder: A handbook for diagnosis and treatment* (pp. 81–115). The Guilford Press.

Beck Institute. (2023, March 7). Cognitive Behavioral Therapy. https://beckinstitute.org

Blomstrand, P., & Engvall, J. (2021). Effects of a single workout on memory and learning functions in young adults - A systematic review. *Translational Sports Medicine*, (4) 115-127.

CHADD. (2021, August 5). ADHD in the News. https://chadd.org/weekly-editions/adhd-in-the-news-2021-08-05/

CHADD. (2019, October 7). The Adverse Health Outcomes, Economic Burden, and Public Health Implications of Unmanaged Attention Deficit Hyperactivity Disorder (ADHD): A Call to Action to Improve the Quality of Life and Life Expectancy of People with ADHD. https://chadd.org/wp-content/uploads/2021/08/CHADD-Health-Outcomes-White-Paper_8-5-21-FINAL.pdf

Centers for Disease Control. (2022, August 9). Symptoms and Diagnosis of ADHD. https://www.cdc.gov/ncbddd/adhd/diagnosis.html

Cotman, C.W., & Berchfold, N.C. (2002). Exercise: a behavioral intervention to enhance brain Health and Plasticity. *Neuroscience*, 25, 295-301.

Coull, J.T., & Cheng, R.K., & Meck, W.H. (2011). Neuroanatomical and neurochemical substrates of timing. *Neuropsychopharmacology*, 36(1), 3-25.

Clough, P.J., Earle, K., & Sewell, D. (2002). Mental Toughness: The Concept and its Measurement. In I. Cockerill (Ed.), *Solutions in Sport Psychology*, 32-46. Thomas Learning, London.

Deuster, P.A., & Silverman, M.N. (2013). Physical fitness: a pathway to health and resilience. *US Army Medical Department Journal*, 24-35.

Feng, L.I., Ren, Y., Cheng, J., & Wang, Y. (2021). Balance Training as an Adjunct to Methylphenidate: A Randomized Controlled Pilot Study of Behavioral Improvement Among Children With ADHD in China. *Frontiers in Psychology*, (11), 1-8.

Goggins, D. (2018). *Can't Hurt Me.* Lioncrest. Carson City, NV.

Healthline. (2023, March 7). Why Being Flexible is Great for Your Health. https://www.healthline.com/health/benefits-of-flexibility

Hove, M. Zeffiri, T.A., Biederman, J., Li, Z. Schmahmann, J., & Valera, E.M., (2015). Neuroimage Clinical. Postural sway and regional cerebellar volume in adults with attention-deficit/hyperactivity disorder May 21;8:422-8. doi: 10.1016/j.nicl.2015.05.005 eCollection.

Jansen, I., Philipsen, A., Dalin, D., Wiesmeier, I.K., & Maurer, C. Postural instability in adult ADHD - A pilot study. Gait Posture. 2019 Jan;67:284-289. doi: 10.1016/j.gaitpost.2018.10.016. Epub 2018 Oct 17. PMID: 30391751.

Kamijo, K., Pomtifex, M.b., O'Leary, K.C., Scudder, M.P., Wu, C., Castelli, D.M., & Hillman,C.H. (2011), The effects of an afterschool physical activity program on working memory in preadolescent children. *Developmental Science*, 14, 1046-1058.

Kazuhiro, T-P., Yus, M., Ruiz-Manrique, G., Lewczuk, A. Arrazola, J., & Montañes-Rada, F. (2018). Amygdala Abnormalities in Adults With ADHD. Journal of Attention Disorder 22(7), 671-678.

Kessler, R., Adler, L., Barkley, R., Biederman, J., Conners, C., Demler, O., Faraone, S. Greenhill, M., Secnik, K., Spencer, T., Ustun, T., Walters, E., & Zaslavsky, A. (2006). The prevalence and correlates of adult ADHD in the United States: results from the National Comorbidity Survey Replication. *American Journal of Psychiatry*, 163(4), 716-723.

Kim, S. M., Hyun, G.J., Jung, T., Son. Y. D., Cho, I., Kee, B.S., & Han, D.H. (2017). Balance deficit and brain connectivity in children with Attention Deficit Hyperactivity Disorder, *Psychiatry Investigation*, 14(4), 452-457.

McGonigal, K. (2023, March 8). The Science of Will Power. www.psychologytoday.com/us/blog/the-science-willpower/201208/smile-your-way-out-stress.

McRaven, W.A. (2017). *Make Your Bed.* Grand Central Publishing. New City, NY.

Nelson, D. (2016, March 20). Self care101: Setting Healthy Boundaries. https://www.dananelsoncounseling.com/blog/self-car-setting-healthy-boundaries/2016.

Ptacek, R., Wissenberger, S., Braaten, E., Klicperova-Baker, M., Goetz, M., Raboch, J., Vnukova, M., & Stefano, G. (2019). Clinical Implications of the Perception of Time in Attention Deficit Hyperactivity Disorder (ADHD): A Review, *International Medical Journal of Experimental and Clinical Research*, 25, 3918-3924.

Raine, L. B., Lee, H.K., Saliba, B. J., Chaddock-Heyman L, Hillman, C.H., & Kramer, A.F. (2013). The Influence of Childhood Aerobic Fitness on Learning and Memory. PLoS ONe 8(9): e72666.https://doi.org/10.1371/journal.pone.0072666

Ratey, J.J., & Hagerman, E. (2008). *Spark*, Little, Brown & Company, NY, NY.

https://www.physio-pedia.com/Romberg_Test

Schlee, T., Neubert, T., Worenz, A., & Milani, T.L. (2012). Children with ADHD show no deficits in plantar foot sensitivity and static balance compared to healthy controls. Research in developmental disabilities. 33. 1957-63. 10.1016/j.ridd.2012.05.020.

Sibley, B.A., & Etnier, J.L. (2003), The Relationship between Physical Activity and Cognition in Children: A Meta-Analysis. *Pediatric Exercise Science*, 15, 243-256.

Slack, L., Maynard, I., Butt, J. & Olusoga, P. (2015). An evaluation of a mental toughness education and training program for early-career English football league referees. *Sport Psychologist*, 29(3). 237-257.

Tajima-Pozo, K., Yus, M., Ruiz-Manrique, G., Lewczuk, A., Arrazola, J., & Montañes-Rada, F. (2018). Amygdala Abnormalities in Adults With ADHD. *Journal of Attention Disorders*, 22(7), 671–678. https://doi.org/10.1177/1087054716629213

Walg M, Hapfelmeier G, El-Wahsch, D., & Prior, H. (2017). The faster internal clock in ADHD is related to lower processing speed: WISC-IV profile analyses and time estimation tasks facilitate the distinction between real ADHD and pseudo-ADHD. *European Child Adolescent Psychiatry*. 26(10), 1177-86.

Wallace, B.A., & Shapiro, S. L. (2006). Mental balance and well-being: building bridges between Buddhism and Western psychology. American Psychology. 61(7), 690-701.

Weiss, M., Hechtman, L.T., & Weiss, G. (1999). *ADHD in Adulthood A Guide to Current Theory, Diagnosis, and Treatment*, Johns Hopkins University Press.

Weissenberger, S., Schonova, K., Buttiker, P., Fazio, Ra., Vnukova, M., Stefano, G.B., & Ptacek, R. (2021). Time Perception is a Focal Symptom of Attention-Deficit/Hyperactivity Disorder in Adults. *Medical Science Monitor*. 17, .

https://hbr.org/2019/the-truth-about-open-offices

https://www.forbes.com/sites/jiawertz/2019/06/30/open-plan-work-spaces-lower-productivity-employee-morale/?sh=5338a33861cd

ABOUT THE AUTHOR

Kari Lewis, ADHD coach and professor emeritus, was the recipient of Teacher of the Year award at a major university where she was a professor in the Health and Exercise Studies Department. She was an educational coordinator for the Multimodal Treatment Study, a national study recognized world-wide as one of the foremost research studies examining the most effective treatment for children with ADHD. She is in private practice as an ADHD coach for children and adults. She has expertise in coaching children to improve time management, organization, and planning for tests and projects. She also specializes in coaching working adults, stay-at-home moms, college students, and highly motivated professionals with ADHD. When coaching she focuses on the total well-being of her clients. Balance, Strength, and Flexibility for those with ADHD: Key components for mental and physical fitness is her first book.